STRESS
LESS

Adams Media
An Imprint of Simon & Schuster, Inc.
57 Littlefield Street
Avon, Massachusetts 02322

First Adams Media trade paperback edition APRIL 2017

ADAMS MEDIA and colophon are trademarks of Simon and Schuster.

For information about special discounts for bulk purchases, please contact Simon & Schuster Special Sales at 1-866-506-1949 or business@simonandschuster.com.

The Simon & Schuster Speakers Bureau can bring authors to your live event. For more information or to book an event contact the Simon & Schuster Speakers Bureau at 1-866-248-3049 or visit our website at www.simonspeakers.com.

Interior design by Michelle Roy Kelly
Interior images © Getty Images/bphillips, Naddiya

Manufactured in the United States of America

10 9 8 7 6 5 4 3 2 1

Library of Congress Cataloging-in-Publication Data has been applied for.

ISBN 978-1-5072-0193-0
ISBN 978-1-5072-0275-3 (ebook)

STRESS LESS

STOP STRESSING · START LIVING

KATE HANLEY

ADAMS MEDIA

New York London Toronto Sydney New Delhi

Dedication

For Lillian and Teddy, who teach me how to be a little bit more present every day.

Introduction

Each day is an opportunity to live your best day. Each day you have the chance to find your peace, your purpose, and to feel good about yourself. These goals (and many others) are absolutely possible if you take charge of your stress. So, the next time stress develops in your life, instead of ignoring it or pushing it down, take the time to look inwardly and ask yourself, *What can I do to change it? How can I stress less?*

After all, everyone has stress, but it is how you choose to cope with it that can make all the difference in your daily life. This helpful guide will give you 100 stress-reducing techniques that will not only calm your body, but your mind as well, and allow you to live your life to its fullest.

Inside you'll find relaxation and calming exercises from meditation to yoga to visualization that can all be accomplished in ten minutes or less. These techniques help you shine the light of awareness on your stress, so you can recognize it, deal with it effectively, and get on with your day.

You'll also discover motivational quotes with each exercise to give you hope, inspiration, and sometimes a bit of laughter (all proven stress-busters!). Use these quotes to give yourself a little boost during the day when you feel stress starting to creep over you.

The majority of the strategies shared here will help you to focus more on yourself—your body, mind, and soul—as a way of shifting your attention away from the things that stress you out. The wonderful paradox is that by focusing on yourself, you also help the people around you.

If you do what it takes to up your contentment and clarity, you'll expose the folks around you to less stress, and you'll inspire them to cultivate their own sense of calm too. It's a lovely ripple effect that just keeps going and going. And it all starts because you picked up this book.

1.
Inhale Calm, Exhale Stress

If you want to conquer the anxiety of life, live in the moment, live in the breath.

—Amit Ray

Here's a way your breath can come to your rescue. Try this:

As you inhale, imagine calm pervading every cell of your body, carried in by your breath.

As you exhale, visualize every iota of angst you've got being drawn out of your body where it can evaporate into the air.

Repeat as many times as you like, but know that even one of these breaths—done with intention—can create a noticeable change.

...

2.

So You Think You Can't Meditate . . .

If you hear a voice within you saying, "You are not a painter," then by all means paint, boy, and that voice will be silenced, but only by working.

—Vincent van Gogh

Many people feel they're "bad"
at meditating, but if you can
count to 10 you can do this.

As you sit someplace quiet, breathing
normally, count each out-breath. When
you get to 10, start again at 1.

When you realize that you're on
27 or that you stopped counting
altogether, start again at 1.

Counting your exhalations gives your
mind something tangible to focus on,
which can help with the "Am I doing this
right?" thoughts that so often pop up.

To really make this practice goof-proof, set a
timer for five minutes so that you don't have
to wonder how much longer to keep going.

...

3.

Go to the Place That Brings You Peace

We're so engaged in doing things to achieve purposes of outer value that we forget that the inner value, the rapture associated with being alive, is what it's all about.

—Joseph Campbell

What's the most relaxing place on Earth for you? Is it in front of a fire in a mountain lodge, or on a hammock near the ocean?

Close your eyes and imagine yourself there, wherever it may be. Really experience it— what can you see, smell, taste, and hear? How does your body feel when you're there?

Because your brain can't perceive a difference between real and imagined relaxation, you can enjoy a truly restorative mini-vacation even if you can't hop a flight or take time off.

...

4.

Just One Question

*To be yourself in a world that is constantly
trying to make you something else is
the greatest accomplishment.*

—Ralph Waldo Emerson

Stress can make everything feel urgent, which makes it hard to decide what to do next.

Step out of the swirl by sitting still long enough to take a nice full breath, in and out.

Then ask:

What do I most need right now?

Whatever answer bubbles up, resist the urge to question or dismiss it. Instead, honor it the best you can in this particular moment.

Asking helps you see that you know more about what you need in any given moment than you might think you do.

...

5.

Cut the String

If you don't like the road you're walking, start paving another one.

—Dolly Parton

Think of a situation that's been weighing you down.

Got it?

Now imagine everything about this circumstance—your boss, your computer, the report you've been working on for weeks—all encased within a big balloon that you're holding the string to in your hand.

And then see yourself letting go of the string and watching the balloon float up and out of sight. (If that doesn't seem to work, take an imaginary pair of scissors and sever that cord once and for all.)

When you find yourself thinking about it again, remind yourself that you've let it go.

...

6.

Take Stock of Your Stress

People become attached to their burdens sometimes more than the burdens are attached to them.

—George Bernard Shaw

If you want to change your relationship to stress, you've got to do a little investigating into how it affects you. Because you can't change a habit you don't know you have.

Where do you hold stress in your body—is it in your jaw, your shoulders, your gut?

What kinds of things do you do to cope— snapping at the kids, yelling at other drivers, eating chips, checking your phone?

This exercise isn't about looking for reasons to beat yourself up. Rather it's about noticing your personal warning signs so that you can start to take countermeasures *before* your stress level is at eleven.

...

7.

Make Doing What You Like a Priority

Only I can change my life. No one can do it for me.

—Carol Burnett

The things you do regularly shape your life much more than the things you do once in a while. So make sure you're regularly doing things that uplift you.

What things do you do frequently that make you feel good? It may be cooking a healthy meal, reading a great book, going for a walk, talking to a friend, or something else.

Let this list help you gauge how you're doing—when you notice that you haven't done anything on it in three days, for example, you know you have to do some re-prioritizing.

...

8.

Change the View

For what you see and hear depends a good deal on where you are standing.

—C.S. Lewis (*The Magician's Nephew*)

Staring at a screen all day makes
your physical world seem small; it
also tires your eyes. Taking a break to
look at something different will shift
your perspective *and* your vision.

Spend the next few minutes looking at
something far away—a painting across the
room, perhaps, or the view out a window.

It will help you remember that there's
more going on in the world than
whatever is two feet in front of you.

...

9.

Watch
the Clouds

One of the best pieces of advice I ever got was from a horse master. He told me to go slow to go fast. I think that applies to everything in life. We live as though there aren't enough hours in the day but if we do each thing calmly and carefully we will get it done quicker and with much less stress.

—Viggo Mortensen

Clouds are nearly always present, yet they are always changing—just like your thoughts. Cloud-watching then can be a great way to develop some objectivity on the nature of your thoughts.

Spend five minutes watching the sky—notice what the cloud shapes remind you of, see if you can detect movement or changes in appearance.

Just as a massive bank of gray clouds will inevitably clear into blue sky, or a cloud shaped like a rabbit will morph into an ice cream cone, your current thought pattern will also transform.

...

10.

Become Curious, Not Furious

When we meet real tragedy in life, we can react in two ways—either by losing hope and falling into self-destructive habits or by using the challenge to find our inner strength.

—His Holiness the 14th Dalai Lama

The next time something really
gets you riled up, try this:

First, notice that you're steamed.
(Awareness is always the first step
in doing things differently.)

Then stay open long enough to ask
questions (before you start yelling or
firing off snippy e-mails) such as:

What's really triggering me here?

*Is there some other way I
could interpret this?*

What if this has nothing to do with me?

When you can manage to tap into curiosity,
you're less likely to judge something
as right or wrong, good or bad. As a
result, you're less likely to overreact.

. . .

11.

Let Yourself
Be Bored

*Chaotic people often have chaotic lives,
and I think they create that. But if you try
and have an inner peace and a positive
attitude, I think you attract that.*

—Imelda Staunton

Boredom gets a bad rap, but it just means "nonstimulated"—which is a much-needed counterbalance to information overload.

Boredom is a chance to be still and observe. It is an invitation for insights and ideas to arise—insights and ideas that you'd be much less likely to generate if you were scrolling through your timeline.

Next time you're feeling bored, notice how long you can sit with it and what feeling or thought comes along to take its place. What changes because you chose to stay present?

...

12.

Give It
a Name

*People have a hard time letting go of their
suffering. Out of a fear of the unknown,
they prefer suffering that is familiar.*

—Thich Nhat Hanh

Instead of ignoring or stuffing down the next emotion that rears its head, ask yourself, *What exactly am I feeling right now?*

Give that feeling a name, and be as specific as possible: Indignation. Resignation. Loneliness. Hurt.

Why? Because in order to accurately identify an emotion, you have to allow yourself to feel it. Actually feeling how you feel is the most efficient way to process those emotions so that they can move on.

...

13.

Listen Better

*Nature hath given men one tongue
but two ears, that we may hear from
others twice as much as we speak.*

—Epictetus

Most of the time when we're talking with someone else, we're not truly hearing what they're saying. Rather, we're thinking about what we'll say in response, or wondering when they'll stop talking so we can speak.

Today, try to really listen. Focus on the other person's words. When you start wanting to finish her sentence, remind yourself that all you need to do in that moment is be receptive.

Training your attention in this way is meditative. As an added bonus, it can also make your relationships better.

...

14.

Find Your Feet

*Be sure you put your feet in the
right place, then stand firm.*

—Abraham Lincoln

Your mind can travel all over the place—past, future, daydreams—but your body is always firmly rooted in the here and now. (No matter how good your virtual reality goggles may be!)

A great trick to help bring your attention to what's happening in this moment is to focus on your body. To make it more specific, focus on your feet.

Where are they right now?
How do they feel?

Your feet are a literal and metaphorical source of support—check in with them whenever you need to come back down to Earth.

...

15.

Pick a Trigger

Love yourself first, and everything else falls into line. You really have to love yourself to get anything done in this world.

—Lucille Ball

Remember the college drinking game where every time a TV character said a certain word, everyone took a drink?

This is a little like that, except it's about becoming more awake instead of more tipsy.

Choose a noise you hear several times a day. A siren. The word "um." Your kids calling you "Mommy." The text message notification sound.

Got one?

Every time you hear that noise for the next twenty-four hours, take a full breath before you do anything else—that's all it takes to turn an ordinary occurrence into a chance to do something nice for yourself.

...

16.

Share Your Experience

Try to understand men, if you understand each other you will be kind to each other. Knowing a man well never leads to hate and nearly always leads to love.

—John Steinbeck

During your next difficult conversation, make it a point to share how you're feeling physically in that very moment, a la:

Even as I'm saying this, I can feel a knot forming in my stomach.

Why? It means you're not trying to direct the conversation toward some end goal. Rather, you're staying present to what's true for you in the moment and inviting someone else into that moment with you. It's about relating, instead of attempting to control—and that helps you connect in a meaningful way.

...

17.

No More
"I'm Fine"

*Being honest may not get you a lot of friends,
but it'll always get you the right ones.*

—John Lennon

The next time someone asks how you are, resist the urge to say "fine" or "busy" and share something that feels true for you at that very moment: hungry, irritated, distracted, happy for no apparent reason, a little punchy.

This gives you an opportunity to check in and see how you're really doing. It also creates an opening to truly connect with the person who's asking—she'll likely be surprised by your answer and will want to either hear more or think a little more deeply about her response when you ask, *And how are you?*

...

18.

Draw Your Inner Critic

Be mindful of your self-talk. It's a conversation with the universe.

—David James Lees

Everyone's got at least one mean voice inside their head. You know, the one who says things like, *What were you thinking? Maybe there's just something wrong with you. You really screwed that one up.*

Pull back the curtain on your inner critic by drawing a picture of her (or him). How old is she? Does she wear glasses? What kinds of clothes do you imagine her in?

If you can personify the voice, you can see that it's not *you*. Which means you'll give her a little less stock the next time she starts in on you.

...

19.

Five
Little Things

*Appreciation is a wonderful thing:
It makes what is excellent in
others belong to us as well.*

—Voltaire

Appreciation is a form of loving attention, and creates an uplifting state of mind that we don't tend to spend much time in. Build your appreciation muscles by taking note of five small things—things you might not otherwise notice—that you appreciate.

In a notebook, number a list 1 to 5. Then, throughout the day, fill each line with one thing that makes your life better—the friend who leaves a funny comment on your Instagram, the sneeze that clears your sinuses, the scent of your neighbor's barbecue, the way your child instinctively reaches for your hand as you walk down the street.

To really boost the benefits, make writing this list a daily check-in for three weeks—about how long it takes to establish a new habit. The more you make note of the things you value, the more things you'll find to appreciate.

...

20.

Natural Sleep Aid: Breathing Out More

A ruffled mind makes a restless pillow.

—Charlotte Brontë

The next time you'd like to pave the way for a peaceful transition to sleep, try this as you're lying in bed:

- Breathe in for a count of three.

- Breathe out for a count of six.

You can lengthen the counts to 4/8 or even 5/10, but longer isn't necessarily better. Stick with what feels best for you.

A big exhalation does three things for your body; it:

- Invites a deep inhalation to flow in naturally

- Engages your diaphragm, which triggers the relaxation response

- Gives your mind something to think about besides your to-do list

Aim for ten rounds.

...

21.

Meditation Made Delicious

One cannot think well, love well, sleep well, if one has not dined well.

—Virginia Woolf ("A Room of One's Own")

"Mindful eating" can sound a bit
. . . wholesome and boring.

But not when you're meditatively
eating a piece of chocolate!

To do it, hold the chocolate in your hand.
Feel its weight. Think of all the people
involved in growing, picking, processing,
and shipping the beans, turning the
beans into chocolate, and shipping the
chocolate to your store. Thank them.

Now savor every facet of eating a tiny
bite—the smell, the taste, the physiological
response you feel in your body. Keep
giving your full attention to the act of
eating until the chocolate is gone.

What did you notice?

. . .

22.

Try
Something New

*Twenty years from now you will be more
disappointed by the things that you didn't
do than by the ones you did do.*

—Mark Twain

What's a skill you've always wanted to learn? Perhaps pasta-making, the tango, maybe embroidery?

Carve out ten minutes today to get started: Watch a YouTube video, do a supply run, book a lesson, or reach out to a friend who can teach you.

The combination of concentration and movement makes learning a new skill a great mind-body practice. It also short-circuits the disempowering story in your head that says, *I don't have time to do the things I want to do.*

(Remember, small steps count; you don't have to master it immediately.)

...

23.

Do Something You've Been Avoiding

If we did all the things we are capable of, we would literally astound ourselves.

—Thomas Edison

Resistance creates stress, the same way dragging an anchor behind a boat creates drag.

What can you do today that you've been putting off? Can you make that phone call, pay that bill, or run that errand?

This isn't about getting something done for the sake of crossing it off your list. It's about unburdening your mind. Doing something that's been nagging at you means you can be done with it.

Be prepared to enjoy a surge of energy that you can then use on something you *do* want to do.

...

24.

Don't Do Something You Don't Want to Do

The art of leadership is saying no, not yes. It is very easy to say yes.

—Tony Blair

Growing up, you were likely told, "Sometimes you have to do things you don't want to." Which is true, but . . .

Doing something strictly out of a sense of obligation, something that otherwise doesn't appeal to you at all, will only deplete you. There are no bonus points for being miserable.

What's one thing in the next week that you really don't want to do at all? Can you simply *not* do it? (Or, if it simply must get done, can you delegate it to someone else?)

...

25.

Pretend You Just Beamed In

Each morning we are born again. What we do today is what matters most.

—Buddha

One of the precepts Buddhism teaches is "beginner's mind"—the ability to see things without preconceived notions. It helps you stay open to things as they actually are instead of how you think they are. It's also a lot harder than it sounds.

For any amount of time today— whether it's one minute or twenty— look at your surroundings as if you're a visitor from another planet who just stepped off her spaceship.

What do you see that perhaps you hadn't noticed before? What insights do you get about family dynamics or office drama when you look at them as an outsider?

...

26.

Do a
Body Scan

*To meditate with mindful breathing is
to bring body and mind back to the
present moment so that you do not
miss your appointment with life.*

—Thich Nhat Hanh

To really immerse yourself in the present moment—and invite all the relaxation that that provides—lie down on your back and get comfortable.

Starting at the top of your head, check in with each body part and see what you can feel there. Take a few or as many as thirty minutes to work down to your toes and then back up to the crown of your head.

No judgments. No rushing. Just paying attention to your own body and accepting exactly how it feels at this particular time.

...

27.

Savor
Something Good

*When you arise in the morning, think of
what a precious privilege it is to be alive—
to breathe, to think, to enjoy, to love.*

—Marcus Aurelius

Your brain is wired to scan for and remember adverse events—this "negativity bias" helped humans adapt to threats in their environment. What was great for our evolution is now a root of stress and anxiety.

To help re-train your brain, dedicate some time to reveling in good memories. Sit quietly and call up a happy moment. Relive that memory in the greatest detail you can muster, and let the good feelings soak into your cells. It will help you appreciate the positive things you experience even more, which boosts gratitude and contentment.

...

28.

Take One Thing Out of Your Backpack

Resentment is like drinking poison and then hoping it will kill your enemies.

—Nelson Mandela

One way you likely contribute to your life feeling stressful is by holding on to things like grudges, hurts, and narratives about how you were wronged. (How very human of you!)

The problem is, as righteous as they may make you feel, these unresolved feelings take up space and zap energy. It's like carrying around a backpack full of rocks. Sure, you're capable of doing it, but what do you get out of it?

What's one small rock you can set down? What trespass can you forgive, or what story can you spin a different way?

...

29.

Two Birds.
One Stone.

*Don't underestimate the value of Doing
Nothing, of just going along, listening to all
the things you can't hear, and not bothering.*

—Piglet (*Pooh's Little Instruction Book*)

Your well-being requires movement and stillness. Here's a way to take care of these two needs in one activity.

Go take a walk to a place you enjoy—a rock by a river, a park bench, or a particular tree. When you get there, sit down and tune in to the sound of your own breathing for five or ten or fifteen minutes. Then get up and walk home. Boom—you've just exorcised and meditated in one fell swoop.

(You could even run an errand on the way home and make that three birds instead of just two.)

...

30.

Love
Your Chores

You can gain more control over your life by paying closer attention to the little things.

—Emily Dickinson

Instead of hating them, dreading them, or ignoring them, use your daily household tasks as a chance to practice mindfulness.

Focus on the swish of the bristles and the transfer of your weight as you sweep; notice the sounds of dishes clinking in the sink and water running as you clean up after dinner; keep one eye on your breath as you fold laundry.

You'll get a refreshed mind and a cleaner house (and lose a lot of angst) in the process.

...

31.

Red Light Relaxation

Breathe. Let go. And remind yourself that this very moment is the only one you know you have for sure.

—Oprah Winfrey

The next time you're in your car, use each red light as a reminder to take one full breath that you pay attention to the whole way through.

Inhale.

Exhale.

How does it change your experience of your commute? Notice any difference in how you feel once you get out of the car and go on with your day?

...

32.

Put Your Phone on Pause

There is more to life than increasing its speed.

—Mahatma Gandhi

Choose one small part of your day to go without your phone—when you walk the dog perhaps, or go to the grocery store, or drive to work (put it in the glove box so you aren't tempted to write a text at a red light).

This way you can have some time each day where you don't have to weigh whether or not to "check in," and you can just sit with these moments of downtime without distracting yourself.

Taking this one regular break will help you choose when to use your phone a little more mindfully and a little less habitually.

...

33.

Use Your Breath to Take a Break

The life of inner peace, being harmonious and without stress, is the easiest type of existence.

—Norman Vincent Peale

Try this breathing pattern for ten breaths:

1. Inhale normally. Exhale normally.

2. Pause.

Begin the next breath *before* you feel desperate for air (meaning, a bigger pause isn't necessarily better).

The beauty of this technique is that it elbows out room for you to rest—to reflect before you make your next move. And that's when you start making decisions that reduce your stress instead of adding to it. Also, no one will notice you're doing it, meaning you can do it anywhere— the train, the dentist's chair, or even in the midst of a difficult conversation.

...

34.

Tell Yourself
Something Kind

*Carry out a random act of kindness, with
no expectation of reward, safe in the
knowledge that one day someone
might do the same for you.*

—Diana, Princess of Wales

There's a reason mindfulness and meditation teach us to detach from our thoughts—so many of them are self-directed and downright mean.

Break the cycle of negative self-talk by thinking of one nice, true thing about yourself, such as: *I have a big heart. I'm doing my best and getting a little better every day. I am so lovable.*

For the rest of the day, repeat it silently any time you notice your thoughts veering in a self-critical direction, or when you simply want a little lift.

...

35.

Take a "Noticing" Walk

Few are those who see with their own eyes and feel with their own hearts.

—Albert Einstein

At some point today, take yourself on a walk where your sole purpose is to see how many interesting, or weird, or beautiful things you can notice.

This isn't about getting your 10,000 steps (although it will help you do that). It's about learning how to observe what's happening in any given moment, instead of getting distracted by, or hung up on, your thoughts.

Whenever you find yourself lost in a train of thought—and you will, because you're human—come back to this question: *What can I see when I allow myself to look?*

...

36.

Soak Up Some
Tree Therapy

*For in the true nature of things, if we rightly
consider, every green tree is far more glorious
than if it were made of gold and silver.*

—Martin Luther

The Japanese have a name for spending time among trees—*shinrin-yoku*, or forest bathing, which has been shown to reduce stress and improve immunity.

Let this exercise be an impetus to spend some time in the company of trees, whether they're in your yard, at your local park, or along a walking trail. The sound of rustling leaves, the woodsy scents, and the dappled light all soothe the soul in a major way—particularly when you use your powers of attention to really appreciate them. Hugging and climbing the trees are optional (but encouraged!).

...

37.

Reset Your Spine

If you ask what is the single most important key to longevity, I would have to say it is avoiding worry, stress and tension. And if you didn't ask me, I'd still have to say it.

—George Burns

The curves of your spine are your body's shock absorbers. Yet spending most of your hours either sitting or sleeping distorts them over time (think of a dowager's hump), leading to stiffness and pain.

To help restore those supportive curves, lie on the floor with knees bent, feet flat on the floor, and the back of your head resting on a book or two (so your forehead is slightly higher than your chin). Put a pillow between your thighs and let the knees fall into each other.

Rest here for ten minutes, feeling your back and core muscles release, which allows the spine to resume its typical shape, which feels like *ahhh*.

...

38.

One Tennis Ball, Three Stress Relievers

A tree that is unbending is easily broken.

—Lao Tzu

A tennis ball can be a great physical stress-buster (and a cheap alternative to a professional massage).

Here are three ways to use one of those fuzzy yellow spheres:

1. Kick your shoes off and stand up. Roll one foot at a time over the ball from toe to heel and back again—call it DIY reflexology.

2. While standing, place the ball of one foot on top of the tennis ball and let that heel drop to the floor for a fabulous calf stretch. Stay five breaths then switch feet.

3. Lying on the floor on your back, place the ball underneath you just to the right of your tailbone. Moving slowly, roll the tennis ball up one side of the spine and back down the other—it'll make you feel at least an inch taller.

...

39.

Meditate Together

Be happy in the moment, that's enough.
Each moment is all we need, not more.

—Mother Teresa

Meditating doesn't have to
be a solitary activity.

Sit with a willing partner someplace that
offers an interesting view—a big picture
window perhaps, or a bench in a busy park.

Take turns calling out the things you notice:
"bird," "cat," "spider web," "empty chip
bag." It's not a race, or a contest. It's simply
a chance to practice noticing what's right
in front of you—without judgment—and
then sharing what you see. It's also a nice
way to relate to someone else—one with no
agenda other than spending time together.

...

40.

Nurture
Your Nature

*Don't judge each day by the harvest that
you reap but by the seeds that you plant.*

—Robert Louis Stevenson

There's something gratifying and soothing about taking care of plants, whether you're a master gardener or just trying to keep a houseplant alive. Having potted plants in the room has even been shown to help hospital patients recover faster!

Take a break from your to-do list today to tend to whatever plants are in your life. Give them some water, clear out the brown leaves, get your fingers in the dirt. It will help you feel grounded and calmer.

...

41.

Take Off
Your Shoes

*What spirit is so empty and blind that it
cannot grasp the fact that the foot is more
noble than the shoe, and skin more beautiful
than the garment with which it is clothed?*

—Michelangelo

Your feet are exquisite sensory input devices—each sole has an estimated 100,000 to 200,000 nerve receptors! However, wearing shoes all the time dulls their ability to transmit information about where you are in space.

At some point in the next twenty-four hours, go barefoot at a time when you would normally wear shoes—watering the garden, fetching the paper from the front steps, walking to the kitchen for a snack. You'll stimulate those nerve endings and give your mind some novel information to process (instead of its usual chewing on the same old worries).

...

42.

Lie on
the Floor

*Your mind will answer most questions if you
learn to relax and wait for the answer.*

—William S. Burroughs

You may not have time for a nap, but you can get a lot of the restorative benefits that a short snooze provides by lying on the floor for a few minutes.

Stretching out on your back on the floor lengthens the spine, creates more space in the torso for breathing, and feels great.

As you lie there, let your hands and feet fall out to the sides and make it your job to continually release any physical tension.

...

43.

Try a Little Kitchen Yoga

Ring the bells that still can ring. Forget your perfect offering. There is a crack in everything. That's how the light gets in.

—Leonard Cohen

Use the time it takes for your coffee to brew, toast to toast, or water to boil for this great-feeling stretch:

1. Place your palms on the edge of the counter and walk your feet back until your arms and spine are fully extended.

2. Bring your feet directly under your hips so your body is making the shape of an upside-down L. Stay here for a few breaths, feeling your spine grow a little longer with each exhale.

This is a great opener for the neck, shoulders, spine, abdomen, rib cage, and back of the legs. And it feels so good that you won't care if your family or your roommates wonder what in the heck you're doing.

...

44.

Don't Just
Sit There

"My dear fellow, who will let you?"
*"That's not the point. The point
is, who will stop me?"*

—Ayn Rand (*The Fountainhead*)

Use your chair as a relaxation tool with this simple stretch that also quiets the mind.

1. Scoot to the edge of your seat, open your feet and knees as wide as the chair seat.

2. Fold forward, resting your torso on your thighs, letting your head and arms dangle down toward the floor.

3. Stay here for a few breaths, feeling your rib cage inflate and deflate with each breath and imagining any stressful thoughts running out of your head and pooling onto the floor.

So you don't disturb the peace you just created, roll up out of this slowly.

...

45.

Rest
Your Heart

Believe you can and you're halfway there.

—Theodore Roosevelt

Although your heart never truly gets time off, you can offer it a little respite by lying on your back on the floor with your calves resting on your coffee table—because elevating your feet means your heart doesn't have to work as hard to pump the blood through the lower body.

Try it tonight—you can make it a mind-body practice by focusing on your breath, or you can do it while watching TV or reading a magazine. Either way, your heart will be happy and your relaxation will rise.

...

46.

The Trustworthy
Downward Dog

*Trust yourself. Create the kind of self
that you will be happy to live with all
your life. Make the most of yourself
by fanning the tiny, inner sparks of
possibility into flames of achievement.*

—Golda Meir

Because it stretches your entire back body, strengthens your upper body, and improves circulation—all in a minute or less—a downward dog a day helps keep the doctor away. And because it literally changes your perspective, it helps refresh your thinking too.

To do it, start on your hands and knees. Tuck your toes under, then straighten your legs and lift your hips up so you make the shape of an upside-down V. Press strongly into your palms to move more of your weight back toward your heels, which are reaching down to the floor. Let your head dangle, feeling every one of its 10 pounds helping your neck and spine grow longer.

To make it more relaxing, rest your forehead (right at the hairline) on a stack of books. To make it more energizing, come forward into the top of a push-up position, or plank pose, as you inhale and move back into downward dog with each exhalation for a total of five cycles. Whichever form you choose, your back, neck, shoulders, heart, and mind will thank you.

...

47.

Refresh
Your Eyes

*The question is not what you look at—but
how you look and whether you see.*

—Henry David Thoreau

From the time you open them in the morning until you close them at night, your eyes are busy taking in the world. Give them—and the visual processing centers of your brain—a break with this easy exercise.

1. Sit or lie comfortably somewhere private with your spine tall but your shoulders melting down your back.

2. Close your eyes and bring the heels of your palms to your eye sockets, applying gentle pressure (it should feel comforting, not oppressive).

3. Stay this way for a minute or two, appreciating the chance to go dark and reboot even in the midst of a busy day.

...

48.

No-Drama
Deep Breathing

*Take the first step in faith. You don't have
to see the whole staircase,
just take the first step.*

—Martin Luther King Jr.

Here are two effortless ways to coax yourself into taking deeper breaths:

1. Sit up straight and rest one hand on your belly, then breathe so that your hand moves away from your spine as you inhale and falls back in on the exhalation.

2. Lie on the floor on your stomach with your forehead resting on your crossed forearms. As you breathe in, feel your belly pressing in to the floor and then receding as you breathe out.

In both positions, aim to take ten breaths.

Which one do you prefer? Which makes you feel more relaxed?

...

49.

Tend to
Your Tootsies

Touch comes before sight, before speech. It is the first language and the last, and it always tells the truth.

—Margaret Atwood

Giving yourself a foot massage is a great way to treat yourself more kindly. It also reduces physical tension and gives you a chance to show some gratitude for the foundation they provide you every day.

Whether you use a fancy cream or a pantry staple (such as coconut oil), rubbing your own feet can help you get more in touch with how your body is feeling—and that helps your mind stop running every which way too.

Try it before bed so that you can hit the hay feeling extra relaxed.

...

50.

Soothe Yourself to Sleep

Sleep is the golden chain that binds health and our bodies together.

—Thomas Dekker

Sometimes sleep is elusive because your thoughts are swirling. Here's a way to draw that energy out of your head and down into the body, which helps you relax:

1. Lying on your back, place one hand on your heart, the other on your solar plexus (just below your breast bone).

2. Breathe naturally, appreciating the comfort that the weight of your own hands provides.

3. After a minute or two, move the top hand down to your belly just below the navel. Continue breathing naturally until you feel yourself beginning to release into sleep.

...

51.

Shout
It Out

*A successful man is one who can
lay a firm foundation with the bricks
others have thrown at him.*

—David Brinkley

Being more mindful doesn't mean you won't ever get angry or upset again. But it can help you express those emotions in a more conscious way.

If you've got some anger to express, let it out with a primal scream in the car. Do it with the intention of getting the feelings out of your body and into the air where they can dissipate.

This exercise gives your frustrations a voice, making it less likely that you'll end up yelling when it comes time to discuss whatever's upsetting you. As a result, you'll be more likely to be heard.

...

52.

Find a Touchstone

Never be in a hurry; do everything quietly and in a calm spirit. Do not lose your inner peace for anything whatsoever, even if your whole world seems upset.

—Saint Francis de Sales

You know a day at the beach or a hike in the mountains makes you feel grounded, calm, and content. While you may not be able to immerse yourself in natural settings every day, you can stay in touch.

Keep a rock in your pocket or in the change compartment of your wallet. Use a beautiful red leaf as a bookmark. Turn a seashell into a paperweight. Then you'll always have a reminder that there's a great big beautiful world right outside—a helpful thought whenever your problems are feeling too big.

...

53.

Zen Up
Your Car

Happiness, not in another place, but this place . . . not for another hour, but this hour.

—Walt Whitman

A car is a utilitarian vehicle—it's how you get to work, run errands, shepherd people you love from here to there. But it's also one of the few places where you are regularly alone, and solitude can be a key component of quieting the mind.

To create more opportunities for rolling serenity, put some things in your car that invite feelings of calm—a pretty crystal for the console, a soothing CD, a picture of a favorite view tucked into your visor. They will serve as reminders to relax a little and go with the flow.

...

54.

Road Grace

Love has within it a redemptive power. And there is a power there that eventually transforms individuals. . . . There is something about love that builds up and is creative. There is something about hate that tears down and is destructive.

—Martin Luther King Jr.

You hear a lot about road rage (and probably experience your fair share of it too). But there's a flip side to this phenomenon that's equally powerful—road grace.

Driving is the perfect opportunity to practice a little compassion in motion: Bless the people who cut you off, the drivers of cars that are nicer or more beat-up than yours, the panhandler at the red light, the person driving slowly in front of you. It doesn't require anything more than a willingness to see the world with loving eyes—a skill that will serve you well in all parts of your life.

...

55.

Make the Most of Mealtimes

You must live in the present, launch yourself on every wave, find your eternity in each moment. Fools stand on their island of opportunities and look toward another land. There is no other land; there is no other life but this.

—Henry David Thoreau

One of the best ways to weave more mindfulness into your life is to combine it with things you already do every day—things like eating.

Decide to eat your next three meals at a cleared-off table—not at your desk, in your car, or as you're walking down the street. Keep your attention on the act of eating—how the food tastes, how it makes you feel.

You don't have to do any special mindful eating practices—just setting down the drive to "get things done" a couple of times a day will help you reset your attention, which naturally helps you be more mindful.

...

56.

Work Out with No Media

The most difficult thing is the decision to act. The rest is merely tenacity. The fears are paper tigers. You can do anything you decide to do.

—Amelia Earhart

It's true; podcasts and playlists are great companions for walks and a TV above the treadmill makes a workout go faster. But when you're busy listening or watching, your mind is doing one thing while your body is doing another. It's not terrible, but it's also missing an opportunity to get these two vital forces on the same page.

Next time you exercise, keep the screens off and rest your attention on what you can feel, see, and hear. If you're outside, take in the scenery. If you're inside, listen to your breath. That way, your mind gets trained too.

...

57.

Where Does It All Go South?

We must be willing to get rid of the life we've planned, so as to have the life that is waiting for us.

—Joseph Campbell

Stress is universal, but it's also personal—
what sends one person into a spiral
will float right by someone else.

What types of situations make your stress
meter spike? Traffic? Coming home to
a messy house? Being criticized?

Use your blossoming mindfulness skills to
pay attention to the things that set you off.
You may be able to discern a pattern that
you can then go about changing. Also,
it's a scientific fact that the simple act of
observing a process can modify its outcome.

...

58.

Listening Meditation

For fast-acting relief, try slowing down.

—Lily Tomlin

Not all meditation has to be internally focused. Placing your attention on what you can hear happening in the outside world is also restful to the mind.

For this exercise, you want to try to discern every little sound that passes your eardrum without giving any noise more attention than another.

To do it, simply sit up tall, close your eyes, and imagine opening your ears. When you get lost in a daydream, guide your attention back to what you can hear.

In addition to being something you can do pretty much anywhere, this practice is great for getting you to see how much more is happening in your immediate environment than you are likely conscious of.

...

59.

Send Someone Some Love

*Do not anticipate trouble,
or worry about what may never
happen. Keep in the sunlight.*

—Benjamin Franklin

Worrying about someone you love disempowers them and puts your focus on what could go wrong instead of what's going right. This is not very helpful.

Here's a way to support someone from afar that's good for them and for you. It's a loving kindness meditation, and it goes like this:

Sitting up tall, close your eyes and call up an image of this person in your mind. Really "see" them as you silently repeat, as many times as feels good:

May you be happy.

May you be free from suffering.

May you be at peace.

...

60.

Check In
with Your Gut

You have brains in your head. You have feet in your shoes. You can steer yourself any direction you choose.

—Dr. Seuss (Oh, the Places You'll Go!)

Most of us have unhelpful voices in our heads (or coming out of the mouths of family or friends) second-guessing our every decision. Yet every single one of us—including you—has a wise voice within. Think of it as your inner Yoda—it is knowledgeable and compassionate, and always knows the best next step.

Anytime you need to make a choice, invite your internal wisdom to weigh in by answering this question:

If there were no wrong choice, the option that feels the most right and true to me is _____.

...

61.

Give Yourself
a Buffer

*Change the way you look at things, and
the things you look at change.*

—Wayne Dyer

Magically create more space in your day by giving yourself more time between tasks. Wake up, leave for work, drive to your appointment, meet your friend at the restaurant, and get in bed all five to ten minutes earlier than you normally would.

When you don't have to continuously recover from the stress of rushing, you'll be more present and effective at whatever you do. Even more importantly, you'll create opportunities for insights to bubble up (and time to actually jot them down so you don't forget them).

...

62.

Admit
a Mistake

*The greatest mistake you can make in life is
to be continually fearing you will make one.*

—Elbert Hubbard

Every single person on Earth makes mistakes regularly. Daily, even. Because every single person on Earth is a human, and humans aren't perfect.

What most humans don't typically do regularly is admit their mistakes—too embarrassing. But here's what else not talking about your mistakes is—stressful. Keeping things hidden takes effort. And it creates fear—what if you get found out?

To uncork some of this angst, make it a point to admit to a mistake in the next twenty-four hours. For example, *Here's what I wish I'd said,* or, *I did this thing that I feel weird about.*

What you confess doesn't have to be big. No matter the size of the slip-up you fess up to, you'll create a noticeable release of tension. It also opens up an opportunity to feel closer to the person you tell.

...

63.

Blow Off
Your Stress

*Some of us think holding on makes us
strong; but sometimes it is letting go.*

—Hermann Hesse

Here's a great stress reducer you can do with your kids: Blow bubbles.

As you do, imagine that you are blowing your concerns into those self-contained spheres. Then watch them float up and away from you and out into the world where they can be absorbed into the atmosphere.

This is a great exercise to use before a nerve-wracking event—a big test or presentation, the first day of school— or at the end of a long day before starting your bedtime routine.

Whenever you do it, do it with the intention of getting the stressors out of your head so that you can create space for more uplifting thoughts.

...

64.

Savor
Your Thresholds

*Life isn't about waiting for the storm to pass
. . . It's about learning to dance in the rain.*

—Vivian Greene

Research has found that your mind organizes memories according to location—which explains why you can walk into a new room and forget what you came in for. In a sense, then, crossing a threshold gives your mind a blank slate.

Maximize this quirk of your psychology by deciding to pause each time you cross a threshold today. Spend one breath surveying the room you're about to step into. Let this moment help you tap into the beginner's mind you practiced in exercise 25, and see what happens differently when you consciously decide to arrive in a new environment without carrying whatever you just experienced along with you.

...

65.

Change Your Seat

You see things; and you say, "Why?" But I dream things that never were; and I say, "Why not?"

—George Bernard Shaw (*Back to Methuselah*)

Holding one position for long periods of time is stressful to your body, which was built for movement.

To break out of a sitting rut, periodically assume a cross-legged position in your chair (as if you were a preschooler sitting on the classroom rug in "criss-cross-applesauce").

You'll open your hips, your ankles . . . and your mind, as the novelty of the position will give it some new sensory input to process. You'll also refresh your heart, which won't have to work as hard to return the blood from your lower extremities as it does when your feet are on the floor.

...

66.

Try a Clearing Exercise

The best way out is always through.

—Robert Frost ("A Servant to Servants")

You can tell yourself to "let it go" all you want, but sometimes you need a physical practice to make that release tangible before you mind can loosen its grip. Here's one from tai chi:

Stand with your feet shoulder-distance apart, knees slightly bent, arms hanging loosely by your sides.

Feel your body from the waist down dropping into the floor, and from the navel up extending up toward the sky.

As you inhale, sweep your arms out and up to chin height, palms facing forward, as if you were going to give an invisible person a hug.

As you exhale, bend your elbows and bring your fingertips toward each other, turning your palms to the floor, and slowly move your hands and straighten your arms down toward the floor, as if you were pushing them through water. Imagine this downward sweep pushing any stress or toxic energy from your body into the ground where it can be absorbed.

Repeat three to five times.

...

67.

Pause for
the Cause

*Sometimes people let the same problem
make them miserable for years when they
could just say, "So what." That's one of
my favorite things to say. "So what."*

—Andy Warhol

Chronic stress is like a dog pulling on a leash—it's constantly trying to drag your attention to the next upset.

To put some slack in your leash, remember that you always have the power to pause. You don't have to immediately jump out of the car as soon as you turn it off, for example. Or answer the phone on the first ring. Or start eating seconds after you sit down. You can pause just long enough to let your mind catch up to your body.

Doing so gives you some breathing space and reduces your odds of getting flustered and of feeling like you're being pulled in a million directions.

...

68.

Say Yes— to *Everything*

What is joy without sorrow? What is success without failure? What is a win without a loss? What is health without illness? You have to experience each if you are to appreciate the other. There is always going to be suffering. It's how you look at your suffering, how you deal with it, that will define you.

—Mark Twain

Resistance is the opposite of acceptance. It can take many forms—judgment, skepticism, complaining, impatience, distraction, a pity party—but acceptance starts with one simple action—saying yes to whatever potentially irritating circumstance is presenting itself to you.

Start cultivating your acceptance muscles by silently saying yes to whatever you encounter today. Dog needs a walk? *Yes.* Empty fridge requires a trip to the grocery store? *Yes.* Kid brings up a sensitive topic that you'd rather not discuss? *Yes.*

You may not be able to immediately cultivate a sense of welcoming for the things you'd rather not deal with, but you can drop some of the immediate armoring that comes with resistance. Saying yes doesn't lighten your load, but it does make it less taxing to bear.

...

69.

Take
Two Trips

*And now that you don't have to be
perfect, you can be good.*

—John Steinbeck (*East of Eden*)

Striving for efficiency is a double-edged sword—while it can save you time and effort, it can also make you feel like you've got to wring every ounce of productivity out of every moment or else you've wasted your time. Talk about stressful!

Just for today, allow yourself to take exactly as much time as a task really needs to be performed well. Got a trunkful of groceries? Take two trips. An overflowing laundry basket? See how long it takes instead of rushing through. The job will still get done, you'll put less pressure on yourself, and you may even build more movement into your day without adding anything else to the list of things you want to accomplish.

...

70.

Let Your Body
Lead the Way

*We cannot direct the wind, but
we can adjust our sails.*

—Bertha Calloway

Feeling disconnected from your body is a source of stress. And it is so easy for the lines of communication between your mind and body to get garbled, particularly with all the mental stimulation coming your way at any given moment.

Today, look to your body (not your calendar or your to-do list) for clues on when to do something. For example, go to the bathroom when you first notice you have to pee (instead of ignoring the urge until you're about to burst). Eat before you're starving (instead of waiting so long that you'll gobble anything in your path). Go to bed when you notice you're tired (instead of forcing your eyes to stay open long enough to watch another episode).

By honoring your body's physical cues, you'll get these two fundamental halves of yourself back on speaking terms.

...

71.

Give Your Neck a Break

We spend precious hours fearing the inevitable. It would be wise to use that time adoring our families, cherishing our friends, and living our lives.

—Maya Angelou

Neck and shoulder tension isn't just from mental stress—it's also a consequence of carrying your head out in front of your body (think of the typical sitting-at-the-computer position with your head craning forward).

When your chin juts forward, your neck and shoulder muscles are forced to do the work of supporting your head that your spine is designed to do. To rediscover the ease that comes from proper alignment when sitting, gently slide your head back until the crown of your head is balanced atop your spine and level your chin. When you find the right spot, it should feel like relief.

Whenever you notice that your chin has floated forward again (and it will—old habits die hard), don't take the bait to be hard on yourself for doing something "wrong." Simply allow it to glide backward once more.

...

72.

Ask for Something You Need

Even if you are on the right track, you'll get run over if you just sit there.

—Will Rogers

Whether it's asking a family member to pass a napkin, a friend for a favor, or your husband to take the kids so you can go to yoga, challenge yourself to open your mouth and make a request today.

This is related to, but different from, asking yourself what you most need in this moment (something you read about in exercise 4)—it's taking the insight you gain from a moment of reflection and saying it out loud.

Making such a request takes awareness. It also takes allowing yourself to be seen as having needs. Which means it can also take courage (especially if you are an "I can handle it" type). But it will bring you comfort.

...

73.

Multitask
with Meaning

*Little minds are tamed and subdued by
misfortune; but great minds rise above it.*

—Washington Irving (*Philip of
Pokanoket: An Indian Memoir*)

There are many instances when trying to do two things at once is ill-advised— when using power tools, for example, or having an important conversation.

But that doesn't mean there isn't a useful place for multitasking, particularly when it comes to taking care of multiple important parts of your life at the same time—for example, walking to do your errands, inviting friends over to cook up several pots of soup that you can all use to stock your freezers, stretching on the nursery floor when your toddler insists that you stay with her until she falls asleep.

Finding meaningful ways to multitask helps you see that it is possible to exercise, connect with friends, take care of your health, parent, and do the other activities that matter to you—and it doesn't require unlimited amounts of time to do it.

...

74.

Walk with
No Destination

*You'll never do a whole lot unless
you're brave enough to try.*

—Dolly Parton

Speaking of multitasking, here's a way to get some movement while also building your relationship with your intuition.

At some point in the next twenty-four hours, take yourself on a walk with no particular destination in mind. Every time you come to a crossroads, take a look in each direction and head the way that's calling to you the most. You're not trying to get anywhere—you're simply letting your gut lead the way.

This exercise is a tangible way to reprogram the well-worn paths of your thoughts, and can open you up to delightful surprises—a coffee shop you've never noticed before, for example, or a chance encounter with a dog or a neighbor who's not on your usual route.

...

75.

Smile
for a While

*A tiny bud of a smile on your lips nourishes
awareness and calms you miraculously.*

—Thich Nhat Hanh

Try this experiment in letting the body lead the mind (instead of the other way around): Bring a small smile to your lips and notice how your thoughts automatically start looking for something to be happy about, the way a dog starts anticipating a walk as soon as you pick up the leash.

This isn't about "putting on a happy face" and pretending to feel a way you don't. It's about nudging your countenance, thoughts, and mood in a positive direction. It's genuine, as opposed to wishful thinking. It's also a way of telling your nervous system that everything is a-okay.

...

76.

Sit
for Two Minutes

*Begin doing what you want to do now. We
are not living in eternity. We have only
this moment, sparkling like a star in our
hand and melting like a snowflake.*

—Sir Francis Bacon

Embarking on (or returning to) a regular meditation practice can be a daunting thought. To get going—right now—put this book down and sit still for only two minutes.

You can focus on your breath (see how many breaths you count in that time), or on the sounds in the room, or the way the light looks. Just choose one focus and stick with it for 120 seconds. (You can even set the timer on your phone to give yourself one less thing to think about.)

This is all it takes to begin. Don't overthink it. Just start.

And . . . go!

...

77.

Find Your Comrades

*In the sweetness of friendship let there
be laughter, and sharing of pleasures.
For in the dew of little things the heart
finds its morning and is refreshed.*

—Khalil Gibran (*The Prophet*)

What stress-reducing activity do you wish you did more regularly? Meditate? Go to yoga? Walk?

Whatever you'd like to do, having a friend or two who support you in doing it will help you stick with it. Today, gather your troops.

You can either find someone to actually do the activity with you, or to be your accountability partner—someone you can text each time you need encouragement or have a success to celebrate or an insight to share. When it comes to making time to do the things that make you feel fulfilled, it definitely takes a village.

...

78.

Watch
a Snow Globe

*Life is a preparation for the future; and
the best preparation for the future
is to live as if there were none.*

—Albert Einstein

Here's a fun way to take a mindfulness break:

Shake up a snow globe and then place your attention on watching the flakes settle until the water is clear again. (There are snow globe apps if you aren't the souvenir-collecting type.)

Not only is it playful and light, but it's a great metaphor for mindfulness— noticing when your mind has gotten churned up and then observing it until it clears. (It's also a great way to start teaching your kids how to meditate.)

...

79.

Focus on What's Right

If you know how to be happy with the wonders of life that are already there for you to enjoy, you don't need to stress your mind and your body by striving harder and harder, and you don't need to stress this planet by purchasing more and more stuff.

—Thich Nhat Hanh

Quick, name three things that are going on right in this moment. Perhaps you're sitting some place comfortable, the sun is shining, and your pet is curled up nearby.

This is an exercise you can do anytime you notice your stress levels rising, because allowing yourself to see what's right in front of you, right now, helps keep you grounded in this moment. And what a relief that is!

...

80.

Ask
a Grandma

*In everyone's life, at some time, our inner
fire goes out. It is then burst into flame
by an encounter with another human
being. We should all be thankful for those
people who rekindle the inner spirit.*

—Albert Schweitzer

Next time you feel like you've messed something up in some way—a curt remark, a typo in an important document, spinach in your teeth—imagine what a loving grandmother might say to you to make you feel better.

This may not be your actual grandmother—if she would say something that reinforces your feeling bad, imagine a more idealized version. The point is to treat yourself to some loving acceptance, making it less likely that you'll embark on a shame spiral.

...

81.

One Breath
a Day

*When you get into a tight place, and
everything goes against you till it seems
as if you couldn't hold on a minute longer,
never give up then, for that's just the
place and time that the tide will turn.*

—Harriet Beecher Stowe

This is for those times when you feel like you can't possibly add one more thing to your daily routine and yet you are deeply craving some relief to your stress.

Commit to paying attention to one full breath a day. Just. One.

If that is your entire stress-reducing practice for a few days, weeks, or months, it's okay. It's enough to keep your seat warm until you're ready to do more and to keep you from feeling like you've completely fallen off the wagon (which is when you're more prone to indulge in unhealthy behaviors that only further your stress).

...

82.

Brush Your Teeth
to Brush Your Teeth

*When you've seen beyond yourself, then you
may find, peace of mind is waiting there.*

—George Harrison ("Within You Without You")

One thing you have to do at least once a day, every day, is brush your teeth. So use this quotidian task as a chance to let go of any agenda or rushing and simply enjoy the experience.

What sensations do you feel? What sounds can you hear? What parts of your body are working and which are simply along for the ride? What does your toothpaste really even taste like?

Getting absorbed in your physical experience will give your mind something to focus on, which will help it quiet down. And you'll get clean, shiny teeth—bonus!

...

83.

Add More of the Good Stuff

The greatest weapon against stress is our ability to choose one thought over another.

—William James

Growing your level of contentment will naturally crowd out some of the habitual stress you may have unwittingly become accustomed to. In order to do that, you need to do a little investigating into what provides that feeling of being at ease.

When are you naturally the most happy and relaxed—what time of day is it, who are you with (if anyone), and what kinds of activities are you doing? Write your answers down and then encourage yourself to both pay more attention to these times when they happen—so that you raise your awareness of this good feeling—and create ways to spend more of your time doing them. It's the equivalent of how eating more vegetables leaves less room in your belly for junk food.

...

84.

Open Up
Your Lens

*Meditation is not a way of making
your mind quiet. It is a way of entering
into the quiet that is already there—
buried under the 50,000 thoughts the
average person thinks every day.*

—Deepak Chopra

There are several exercises in this book that talk you through narrowing your focus—choosing one thing, such as your breath, or the clouds, to pay attention to.

This exercise takes the opposite track—for the two minutes after you finish reading this, plop yourself down somewhere and simply take in every visual detail you can. Be receptive to everything, from the dust motes in a beam of light to the wail of a siren.

You don't need a laser beam focus on everything you notice—make your vision softer and wider, as if you were pulling back the zoom on a camera. Simply see what happens.

...

85.

Put 'Em Up

Once you choose hope, anything's possible.

—Christopher Reeve

Raising your arms above your head does many wonderful things—it opens the chest, shoulders, and neck (all the areas that get congested by sitting and looking at a computer or phone), creates more space in the torso for your lungs and digestive organs to have the room they need to function optimally, and strengthens your core muscles. And yet, we rarely do it. Let's change that.

1. Stand up with your feet at hip distance. Raise your arms out straight in front of you at shoulder height.

2. Interlace your fingers and turn the palms to face out. Now raise your arms until your palms point straight at the ceiling.

3. Lift your shoulders up toward your ears, and then let them drop down so that your neck is long and tall.

4. Finally, lift your ribs and spine up off your pelvis so that you unfurl to your tallest height.

5. Stay for three breaths, and repeat a few times throughout the day.

...

86.

Get It Out
of Your Head

*When I let go of what I am, I
become what I might be.*

—Lao Tzu

Here's a tried-and-true technique taught in Julia Cameron's classic self-help tome, *The Artist's Way:* Start your day with some no-holds-barred journaling. Set a timer for three minutes and write down absolutely *anything* that pops into your head, even if it's *I have no idea what to write.* Don't take your pencil off the page until time is up.

The idea is to give every fear, concern, and complaint a place to go so that you don't have to carry them around. Also, putting them on paper helps you see that your thoughts are separate from you, and that you can decide if you want to put stock in them or not. It also invites your inner wisdom to chime in.

...

87.

Focus on People's Goodness

I learned that courage was not the absence of fear, but the triumph over it. The brave man is not he who does not feel afraid, but he who conquers that fear.

—Nelson Mandela

Having a worldview that "people suck" may seem like a smart, protective move, but it leads to feelings of disconnection—which is alienating and, ultimately, stressful.

The truth is, people are more alike than they are different, but our brains are wired to scan for the differences instead of the similarities.

Just for one day, look for the goodness in every person you encounter. This is something you likely do naturally with your kids or your pets—see their good qualities and love them for it. Can you do it for the clerk at the grocery store? The crossing guard at your kid's school? The neighbor you're having a squabble with?

You'll train yourself to see how all people have an inherent goodness, even if they look, act, or think differently than you do. And *that's* when you start to feel connected. Which feels great.

...

88.

Enough Is Enough

It is not a daily increase, but a daily decrease. Hack away at the inessentials.

—Bruce Lee

A great place to start building your contentment muscles is around food. As anyone who has overeaten to the point of feeling sick can attest, there is a definite moment when you have had "enough" food. Today, experiment with determining when that moment is.

Empty, your stomach is about the size of your fist (although it can expand after a big meal). So practice serving yourself portions that are small enough to fit inside your two cupped hands—typically, the size of a cereal bowl. After you've finished that portion, sit for one full minute before deciding if you need more.

Even if you end up eating as much as you otherwise would have, taking the pause to check in with yourself will help you calibrate what "enough" means to you, and coax you to pay more attention to what contentment feels like in your own body.

...

89.

Working with Restlessness

Your vision will become clear only when you look into your heart. Who looks outside, dreams. Who looks inside, awakens.

—Carl Jung

Impatience is, at its core, wanting things to be other than they are now. This isn't inherently bad—a desire for something better can be a great impetus for making needed changes. But it can become a habit that keeps you locked in a state of judging things as being "wrong."

The irony is that the swiftest way to make change is to fully accept where you are now. When you notice your impatience rising today, ask yourself:

- *What am I resisting?*

- *How can I accept what's happening instead of labeling it as "bad"?*

- *Is this situation truly bothering me, or might it be something else?*

...

90.

Take Stock of Your Stress

*The world breaks every one and afterward
many are strong at the broken places.*

—Ernest Hemingway (*A Farewell to Arms*)

Think about a recent stressful situation,
and ask yourself these questions:

- *What were the triggers that set me off?*

- *What about those triggers really bothered me?*

- *What thoughts was I having when I was agitated?*

- *How empirically true are those thoughts?*

- *What's a different way of looking at the situation?*

- *What things could I have done either
before that moment or in that moment that
would have helped me feel better?*

- *What do I want to do the next time
I'm in a similar situation?*

Use your answer to that last question to write a
statement (actually write it on an index card
or on a sticky note) that you can refer back to
the next time you're in a similar situation.

...

91.

Use Music
As Medicine

*Music expresses that which cannot be said
and on which it is impossible to be silent.*

—Victor Hugo

You know that listening to music can lift your mood, give you energy, or take your edge off. You may not know that it can also be a health tonic—researchers have found that listening to music triggers the release of endorphins, which likely explains why science has found that listening for one hour each day can reduce pain levels by as much as 20 percent.

Today, devote your full attention to a piece of music you love—during your commute, as you do the dishes, or as part of a wind-down routine before bed. Bonus points for singing along (as singing has been shown to reduce cortisol).

...

92.

Have
More Fun

*There is no duty we so much underrate
as the duty of being happy.*

—Robert Louis Stevenson

You can't be having fun and feeling stressed at the same time—fun is light, enjoyable, and energizing. It broadens your horizons, where stress is depleting and limits your focus to that which is urgent.

So . . . how much fun have you been having lately?

If the answer is none, or not enough, look at your calendar for the next week and find a time to do at least one thing just for recreation—play tennis with a friend, go salsa dancing, visit a used bookstore. Having it scheduled will help you relax a little the rest of the week, knowing that you're doing something to tend to your happiness.

Also, encourage yourself to weave smaller bits of fun into your everyday experience—eat dinner on the patio, drive home the pretty way, play with the kids on the playground instead of checking your phone. These moments will lift your spirits and make everything else you do feel a little more effortless.

...

93.

Create Space for Stress Relief

Nothing can bring you peace but yourself.

—Ralph Waldo Emerson

Peace doesn't happen by accident—
it's something you have to clear some
space for and invite to come sit by you.

Carve out an area in your home that's
devoted to nothing other than chilling out.
If you have a whole room, fabulous, but it
could be someplace small—one particularly
comfy chair with a cozy throw, or the
windowsill above your kitchen sink that
you look at every time you do the dishes.

You don't have to make it Pinterest
perfect, just spend a few minutes de-
cluttering this spot and gathering a few
items that will lend it a supportive air.
Now you'll have a place to go whenever
you want an inviting space to just be.

...

94.

Three-Minute Check-In

I have learned over the years that when one's mind is made up, this diminishes fear; knowing what must be done does away with fear.

—Rosa Parks

Instead of diving into your inbox first thing and going straight into reaction mode, start your day knowing what's most meaningful by asking yourself these two simple questions:

1. *What's most important to work on today?*

2. *What feels good to work on today?*

Sometimes the answers will align, and sometimes they'll be wildly different. But by tending to your answers, when you lay your head on the pillow tonight, you'll know you spent time prioritizing the important over the merely urgent— and that's a recipe for resting well.

...

95.

Set
an Intention

You can, you should, and if you're
brave enough to start, you will.

—Stephen King *(On Writing)*

An intention is like a force field that you set around your thoughts—giving you a focus that keeps your mind from spinning in multiple directions. To set one for yourself, create a simple statement about how you want to be (don't get too attached to a specific result, or else your subconscious may not buy it).

- *Today, I'll stay curious when I get challenged.*

- *I look for the good in every situation.*

- *I find opportunities to do good.*

Whenever things get stressful, you'll have a safe harbor to return to.

...

96.

Mindful Technology

Few of us ever live in the present. We are forever anticipating what is to come or remembering what has gone.

—Louis L'Amour

As wonderful as technology is, it's also highly addictive and can keep you in a reactive state—*did my phone just buzz?*

Take a moment to take stock of your technology use. Is there one simple change you could make that would help you be more conscious of how and when you interact with it? Possibilities include:

- Turn off push notifications.

- Use an old-school alarm clock instead of your phone.

- Power down all your devices at least thirty minutes before bed.

- Decide to check your e-mail only once an hour, or at a few specific times a day.

- Decide on something you'll do before checking your phone, such as taking three breaths or doing ten jumping jacks.

Just choose one tactic you can commit to. You want to set yourself up for success—too many rules may make you feel intimidated and unmotivated.

...

97.

Open
Your Hips

*Remember always that you not only
have the right to be an individual; you
have an obligation to be one.*

—Eleanor Roosevelt

Your hips are amazing joints that provide 360 degrees of motion (think of a roundhouse kick). Yet you likely only move them in one plane—front to back—while sitting, walking, or running.

Here's a simple stretching routine that will improve range of motion in your hips and ward off back pain and pelvic floor issues. Do it while you're watching TV instead of sitting on the couch.

Cobbler's pose: Sit on the floor with knees bent and soles of the feet touching. If your knees are far from the floor, prop them up with throw pillows. Stay one or two minutes, allowing your knees to gradually release farther down toward the floor.

Straddle pose: Open your legs into a wide V shape, with your toes pointed up at the ceiling. Place your hands on the floor just behind your hips and press into them to lift your chest. Knees can be bent if the backs of your legs are tight, but imagine them releasing incrementally down toward the floor as you stay for a minute or two.

Hero's pose: Kneel on both knees and draw yourself up high—as if standing on your shins—with toes untucked. Keep your knees together and open the feet wide apart, then sit down in between your feet. If your buttocks don't reach the floor, sit on as many books as you need to be able to stay for one or two minutes. This gets your hips internally rotated and is a great stretch for your quads, knees, and ankles, and the tops of your feet.

...

98.

Press Away
the Pain

*Every strike brings me closer
to the next home run.*

—Babe Ruth

Whether you had one glass of wine too many or your stress has taken root in your body as neck and shoulder tension, a headache is a sign that you need a little TLC. Here's an easy way to give some to yourself.

When you notice the first stirrings of a headache, apply pressure to the spot on your hand that's associated with relief of headaches in Traditional Chinese Medicine. To find the point, extend all five fingers of your left hand—it's located within the small mound of flesh located at the bottom of the crease between your thumb and index finger. Press the top of this spot with your right thumb and the underside of it with your right index finger, squeezing them in toward each other, and hold for several breaths. Then repeat on the right hand.

This is also a great technique when you notice yourself overthinking, as stimulating this point is thought to draw energy out of your head and down into your extremities where it can be released.

...

99.

Get
in Touch

*A man who wants to lead the orchestra
must turn his back on the crowd.*

—Max Lucado

Whenever you need to calm down, rest your hand on your stomach or your heart to draw your focus down, away from your head and its litany of thoughts, and into your body, where you are always in the present moment and where your inner wisdom resides.

It's a small movement with big results—so small, you can do it even in a meeting or while riding a crowded train—because it helps you use your whole being to handle whatever stressor is at your door.

...

100.

Let It
Out

Your time is limited, so don't waste it living someone else's life. Don't be trapped by dogma—which is living with the results of other people's thinking. Don't let the noise of others' opinions drown out your own inner voice. And most important, have the courage to follow your heart and intuition. They somehow already know what you truly want to become.

—Steve Jobs

When a difficult client, cranky coworker, or overbearing family member threatens to ruin your day, de-stress with this exercise derived from yoga's lion pose.

1. In an empty room (or even your car), sit up tall. Clench your fists, squeeze your eyes shut, and tighten all the muscles in your face.

2. Next open your eyes and mouth wide, splay your fingers, and stick out your tongue and exhale with a loud whisper sound—like a lion with laryngitis.

This move drains tension out of the body, expels anger, and gives your frustration a voice, all without lashing out at someone and potentially making the upset worse.

. . .